The Simple Truth

A Basic Guide to Metaphysics

By Mary-Alice Jafolla

Unity Books
Unity Village, Missouri

Cover and Illustrations
By Carolyn Bowser

Illustration on page 8
By Betty Chaisson

Second printing 1983

Copyright © 1982 by Unity School of Christianity
Library of Congress Catalog Card #81-69084
ISBN: 0-87159-146-4

Contents

A Letter from the Author 5

What Is God? 9

Spirit, Soul, and Body 15

Everyone Is Equal 21

I Am a Child of God 23

God's Promises 27

Where Is Heaven? 29

How Do I Find God? 31

How Do I Pray? 33

Who Is Jesus? 39

Who or What Is Christ? 41

What Is the Holy Spirit? 43

What Is the Bible? 45

God's Laws 49

I Create with My Thoughts and Words 53

Yes and No 55

There Is Good in Everything 59

Don't React! 61

We Must Not Condemn Others 63

Let's Talk About Forgiveness 67

It's Good to Be Thankful 71

I Am Prosperous 75

God Doesn't Know About Sickness 79

Love Holds the World Together 83

What Is This Thing Called Faith? 85

Why Am I Here? 89

I Will Become New 93

A Letter from the Author

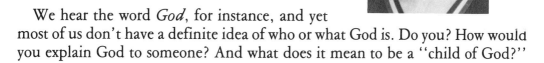

Dear Friend,

This book is written in the hope that it will answer some of the important questions you probably have always had in your mind.

We hear the word *God*, for instance, and yet most of us don't have a definite idea of who or what God is. Do you? How would you explain God to someone? And what does it mean to be a "child of God?"

We also hear the names *Jesus* and *Christ*. Do you know the difference between these two words? And what about the *Holy Spirit?* That's a confusing one, isn't it? Maybe this book will help you to understand such things.

Have you ever wondered why we say everything is good and yet there seems to be so much "bad" around us? Or why something "bad" happened to you?

Or how about the big question everyone has asked, "Why am I here?" You are not alone in wanting a good answer to that one! Perhaps you will have a better idea of why you are here after reading this book.

It is good to ask these questions. It is good to look for their answers and to do some thinking about them. The surprising fact is that the answers to the most important questions in the world are usually very simple. We often try to look for complicated reasons and hidden meanings. Sometimes we feel that if something is of great importance it has to be difficult to understand. But this isn't so.

No doubt you have many questions about yourself and your relationship to the universe and to God and to other people. While this book cannot answer every question you might ask, I hope it will answer some of the most important ones. As you journey through its pages you may come to see that the answers to your questions are not as difficult as you might imagine, and that the ''biggies'' of life can be reduced to a very *Simple Truth!*

Mary-Alice Jafolla

What Is God?

The Biggest Question First

We might as well jump right in and start with the biggest of the ''biggies'': What is God? This and ''why am I here?'' are probably the two most important questions anyone can ever ask. Let's see if we can get a good idea of what God is so that whenever we think or talk of God we have something definite in our minds.

People say that to try to define God is to limit His full range. In other words, if we can define something, it means we can see its limits, its beginning and end. It means we are saying we know all there is to know about the subject. And this criticism of the attempt to define God is probably a good one, because we cannot know all there is to know about God.

But, while we may not be able to know and understand *all* of what God is, we can at least know and understand *some* of what God is. And these ideas will help us to find more and more of the meaning of God as time passes.

Everything Is Part of God

Everything you see, from the book you are reading to the farthest star, is part of God. You are part of God, and so are your friends and all the people on Earth. In fact, the Earth itself is part of God. Even the things we cannot see, such as

9

sounds, smells, and feelings, are part of God. *Everything* is part of God.

There is no place, from the tiniest part of your body to the largest mountains on the moon, where God is not. And because all people and all things are part of the *one* thing we call God, this means that you are related to all people and all things. It is as if we all have the same parents. And in a way we do, because God created us all.

We often refer to God as our Father, or Father-Mother, but God is not a person. No one can really completely say what God is because God is so vast, and there is so much about life that we do not yet know. But we do know that God is everywhere and has created everything and everyone, and that He wants all of creation (including you) to be perfect.

God never changes, because God is Truth, and Truth is always perfect. We only see a very small part of this Truth which is God. We only see some of the grains of sand on a beach, don't we? And yet we know what a beach is. We only see some of the water in the ocean, and yet we know what an ocean is. It is the same with God. We know Him because we know ourselves and our school and our friends and our toys and our parents. God cannot be separated from His creation.

Adults sometimes make the idea of God very difficult and confusing, when it is really very simple. God is everything—everything! And it is *all good!*

We also know that God knows everything. There is not a fact or an idea that God does not know. God has all the answers to every question and problem that can ever arise.

Ideas Come from God

Since we are part of God, our minds are part of God's mind. This is where all ideas come from. In other words, there is one huge God-Mind, and everyone's mind is part of it. We can receive wonderful ideas and answers from God's mind when we keep our thoughts on God and His great goodness.

The perfect intelligence of God is not only working in your brain, it is found within every tiny cell of your body. God's intelligence directs all of the marvelous tasks of each cell so that the entire body runs perfectly. Each cell knows exactly what to do and how to do it. The "wizard" (God Power) within you knows how to take the good and nourishing food you eat and turn it into strong, healthy body tissues and blood. It knows how to make your heart beat and your lungs breathe. It does these marvelous things without your being aware that it is doing them.

Wouldn't it be impossible if each time your heart were supposed to beat, *you* had to remind it to do so? Or each time your lungs needed air, you had to tell them to inhale? Have you ever thought of all the fantastic things that go on in your body which never need your direction?

No scientific genius in the entire world can do the amazing things that each cell of your body can do. It is a good idea to spend a few minutes each day thinking of how perfectly and how intelligently you are made. Try to realize what kind of mind God must have to be able to create something as wonderful as a human being!

The Beginning

You began as an *idea* in the mind of God. Before anything can be created or built there has to be an idea or a design for it first. You cannot build a bookshelf, put together a puzzle, or construct a bridge without having the idea or plan for it.

And that is what happened with you, too. God planned you. He had a perfect idea of what you should become. And then He created you according to that plan. No two plans are ever the same, and no two people are ever the same. But we must remember that, although we each appear to be different, we are all part of the one God.

You know now that God is everything and everywhere, and that God is also all of the knowledge and ideas that ever existed or ever will exist in the future. So, we can say that God is really a Mind, and that because God is everywhere, His supreme intelligence is everywhere too.

In addition to being everywhere present (another word for this is *omnipresent*) and all-knowing (another word for this is *omniscient*), God is also all-powerful (*omnipotent*). There is not a single thing that you can think of that is too difficult for God to do. Isn't that exciting? *Nothing* is impossible for God. His power is so great and so strong that it can do anything.

This power of God is a force which pushes toward good for each of us and for the entire world. God created all of us and the world, and it is only natural that He loves what He creates. He moves always in the direction of good and perfection for His creation.

God's Way Is Best

Sometimes people forget they are part of God. They try to do things their way, and so they block the mighty flow of God's power to do good. If you will keep your mind on what God wants instead of what you want, the very best and most wonderful things will happen in your life, because God's wish is always for your very best. And He has the power to do the best if we human beings will do our best to become as perfect as God intended us to be.

Do you want some examples of this mighty power of God? It is God's power that holds the planets in their orbits around the sun; it is God's power that makes the tides of the ocean rise and fall; it is God's power that makes the flowers come out of the ground each spring; and it is God's power that keeps you alive and well.

Begin today to look for signs of God. See Him in all people and in all things. Sense His masterful intelligence at work, making plants and trees grow, and making your body function as it does. Feel God's supreme power in the wind, in the turning of the Earth from day to night, and in the little weed that pushes up through the cracks in the concrete of a wall or sidewalk.

See how many ways and in how many places you can find evidence of God. The more you look, the more you will find it. And when you find it, realize how fortunate you are to be part of this God who can create such miracles. Doesn't it feel good? Doesn't it make you happy to know God?

Spirit, Soul, and Body

Spirit Is the Real You

Have you heard the words Spirit, soul, and body and wondered what they mean? We especially seem to confuse *Spirit* and *soul*. Well, they are two very different things, as you will soon see.

Your *Spirit* is the real you. It is the perfect part of you that is God. Since this real you is perfect, it never changes. Spirit is the part of you that knows it is God. It is the part of you that you will always be trying to keep in touch with because it will guide you and create the best for you.

When you think about the wisdom of God and really feel how wonderful it is, you are making contact with the spiritual part of yourself.

It is your Spirit that loves everyone and everything because everyone and everything are part of God. All people have the same perfect Spirit as you do. Every human being who ever lived has this perfect part of him or her, no matter how otherwise it may appear to us.

What Is the Soul?

The *soul* changes. Your soul is made up of your thoughts and feelings, and everything that is included in the mind. The soul decides the way you act and what you say. Although it cannot be seen, it determines everything about your

15

life and makes you what you are.

Let's picture the soul as a swinging door. It can go in or out. If we think inwardly—in other words, if we turn our thoughts to the perfect God part of us—we will receive all the marvelous ideas we need in order to be happy and well. When we do this, we say we are turning our souls inward to Spirit.

The soul can also turn to the outer world—to all the things and people and events around us. When the soul focuses on these things, it often receives false information. Something can seem "bad" or make us unhappy. But the Truth is that we are perfect, and all things are good because all things are God. The trouble is that not everyone always *acts* as if he were God, so the God-self of that person cannot show through. But it is still there. (Were there ever times you were mean to someone or said an untrue thing? If you did, you were not letting your God-self show through, were you?)

You can see, then, that we cannot always rely on what we see and hear in the outer world. Since we would naturally want to fill our souls with only Truth, we must turn to that God-self inside us for correct information.

There is a reason why the soul must be filled with the right things: *You will become exactly what is in your soul!* This is such an important truth to know that you should say to yourself: *I become what is in my soul.*

Let's see just what this means. Whatever you really believe and feel strongly about and think about over and over will somehow happen in your life. You see, your body and the events in your life are the results of directions from your soul. The soul is like a factory. It doesn't care *what* it produces; it just produces. But, it can only produce what it has been told to produce.

For instance, if you really believe that you are not smart—that you will get poor grades in school—the soul will find a way for you to get poor grades. If you really believe that your teacher doesn't like you, your soul will see to it that you behave in such a way that the teacher may not like you.

Does all of this sound hard to believe? Does it seem impossible that the way you feel and look and act are the results of what your soul created for you? Does it sound unbelievable that the things that are happening in your life are caused by your own thoughts and beliefs? You can prove it for yourself. Later in the book you will learn how.

About the Body

Your *body* is a place where God lives. It also is the home of your soul. People all over the world build beautiful churches, temples, and cathedrals, which they admire and respect as ''God's House.'' But they often forget that God also dwells within the human body. We would not throw garbage and trash into one of these man-made houses of God, would we? But many of us throw garbage and trash into our bodies! When we eat the wrong foods we do just that—we thus damage the temple that God Himself constructed. Because your body is a temple for God, it should be as perfect as it can be. We wouldn't want to put God in an old shack, would we? That's why we should eat only good, nutritious foods, get a lot of healthful exercise, and have enough rest. This is what the body likes.

You must remember, however, that the body, in addition to being a place where God lives, is the outer reflection of your soul. If your soul is turned inwardly to God and is filled with happy, loving thoughts, the body will be well and happy too. It always faithfully carries out the instructions the soul gives to it.

It's Review Time

Are you clear on what Spirit, soul, and body are? Let's have a quick review. Spirit is your perfect, real self which is part of God. Everyone's Spirit is perfect because it is God.

Your soul is everything that goes on in your mind—your thoughts, beliefs, attitudes, and feelings about things. The soul can "tune in" to your Spirit or it can "tune in" to the world. It dictates your entire life, and so it should be happy and loving.

Your body is the home of God. It is important to keep it well and strong.

Body, soul (or mind), and Spirit—these are the three parts of you. Think about each part and try to see how it works in your life.

If you understand the difference between soul and Spirit, you are making good progress. And do not forget to take good care of the body by feeding it properly and getting good exercise. The human body is one of God's great creations. He wants you to keep it perfect for Him and for you.

Everyone Is Equal

You are Needed!

The universe would not be complete without you. You are very important to God. Everyone is important to God.

Do you remember that God is in every person? This is true. It doesn't matter what color of skin or hair a person has, or what church, temple, or mosque he worships in, or what school he goes to, or where he lives, or what language he speaks. Every human being was created by God.

We should never forget that no matter how different someone seems to us, these differences are only on the "outside." Inside there is always the perfect Spirit which is part of God.

This is something not many people know yet. When a lot of people know what you now know about God being in all people, there will be no more wars and crimes and hatefulness in the world. Someday the world will be like that. Everyone will recognize God in everyone else, and our world will be loving and peaceful.

Laws and governments cannot make this happen. It will happen when each person knows that God is within him. You can help the world by knowing this great Truth about yourself and others and living every day being aware of God. Soon others around you will begin to understand, too, until the love and happiness and kindness you started will circle the Earth!

The Power Is at the Center

Did you ever toss a stone into a lake or a pond and notice the ripples it makes? The rings go out, out, and out, don't they? So much action from one small stone at the center! This is just the way you can help to change the world and make it even better than it is. You will be like the little stone at the center, and your good thoughts and actions will reach out in ever-increasing circles as more and more people see what beautiful changes are happening.

Isn't it exciting to know what one person can do? See how many ways you can think of to bring more peace, love, and happiness into the world right where you are. And since everyone is just as much a part of God as you are, it won't be long before others will be joining in and spreading the circle even wider.

I Am a Child of God

Our Father Loves Us

You often will hear people refer to themselves as children of God, or call God their Father. We use these words because it is probably the simplest way to describe our relationship to God.

When we say that God is our Father, we mean that He created us. He created the original idea of us. And, just as any good father does, God gives us all His wonderful gifts. Everything He has is ours.

God does not directly give us presents of things, such as money or clothes. He gives us something much better than that. He gives us minds filled with ideas for us to use and to have better lives.

These ideas from God are called *spiritual gifts*. They are our true inheritance from God. The more we realize we have these spiritual gifts the more we will use them to make good things happen in our lives. We discover these gifts when we listen to our inner voices.

The Wasteful Son

There is an excellent story in the Bible that shows us clearly how we inherit God's gifts. It is found in Luke, chapter 15, verses 11-32, and it is called the story of ''The Prodigal Son.'' (The word ''prodigal'' means wasteful.)

A man had two sons. The younger one, after asking his father to give him his full share of his inheritance, took the money and went away. He soon wasted all of the money on foolish things and, when a shortage of food occurred in that land, had no money to buy anything to eat; and so he began to starve.

He realized that things were much better back at his father's house, and he decided to return home. Feeling ashamed and sorry for having been so foolish, he asked his father to treat him not as a son but as a servant. But the father was so happy to have his son back that he gave him a ring, beautiful clothes, and had a great feast prepared to celebrate.

The older son became jealous of all the attention and gifts his brother was receiving. He said it wasn't fair—that he had been a loyal son and hadn't run away as his brother had, and yet he had never been given such gifts and celebrations. But his father explained to him that his thinking was wrong. He told the older son that he was always a part of him, and that everything he owned was his for the asking.

His Gifts Are Ours

Do you see what happened? The older brother had access to those wonderful things all the time, but he never took advantage of them! This is exactly what we do when we don't take advantage of God's spiritual gifts.

Are you using your spiritual gifts? Do you listen for the great ideas that God has for you? Do you use your talents and abilities in the best ways? When we know we are part of God and all His goodness, we begin to act like children of God. We begin to take advantage of the divine gifts we have inherited.

And we do not want to become like the younger brother—the prodigal son. This happens when we waste our thoughts, words, and activities on foolish things.

Read the story of ''The Prodigal Son'' in the New Testament. Think about the two brothers. Try to feel how each of them felt. Which one are you most like? The one didn't realize how fortunate he was, and the other one wasted his gifts.

Then think of the father and how he loved both of his sons and gave them everything he had. This might give you some idea of your relationship to God who, because of His great love for you, has already given you everything He has.

God's Promises

He Always Keeps His Word

It is nice to know that there is one thing in the world we can always count on: God never breaks His promises!

Do you know that God has made promises to us? He has. And He always keeps them. Always! Would you like to know what these promises are?

God's promises are sometimes called His laws. And God's laws never change. We can always rely on them. Everything functions according to God's law. The tides rise and fall according to God's law. An oak tree grows from an acorn because of law. If you plant some radish seeds, you will get radishes and not carrots, because seeds must grow according to law.

God's promise to the world is that everything functions according to perfect law and for good. The Bible tells us that the rainbow is God's symbol of His promise. Each time we see a rainbow we can stop for a minute and smile, because we know what it means.

We Have to Do Our Share

While it is true that we can always count on God to keep His promise to us, we have to do *our* share too. It is only fair that we should keep our part of the contract. Our part includes making good use of our inheritance from God, and doing our best every day to follow God's laws. We need to think right thoughts, say right words, do right things, and eat right foods. We know that when we do all these things we are obeying the laws God created for us. And when we obey His laws we can always expect that He will do His share.

We will learn more about God's laws later. This lesson is to help you understand that God can never break His promises to you. He is always doing His share. Are you doing yours? We must be fair, you know!

Where Is Heaven ?

Heaven Is an Inside Job

You can search the universe forever and never find a place called heaven. Do you know why? Because heaven is not a place. It cannot be seen or visited. That's because heaven is a state of mind. *Heaven is in you!* It is in everyone.

When we are aware that we are part of God, and when we live our lives as if we really believe it—obeying the laws and will of God—we experience heaven.

In other words, when we do our best to let God be Himself in us, that is heaven. It is always right here, waiting. We don't have to go anyplace to find it. We only have to wake up to the fact that wherever we are God is, and that means we live in heaven right now.

Heaven Is Where You Are

You have always lived in heaven. You just didn't realize it. But now you do. And you will begin to see how beautiful, good, and loving your life is.

Once you know you carry heaven inside you, you see the world as God sees it. And God sees everything as perfect. God sees with *your* eyes and hears with *your* ears. God's ideas flow into *your* mind. God uses *your* hands and expresses Himself through *your* body. It is your job to realize this. And when you do—that's heaven!

How Do I Find God?

He Is Everywhere, Always

God is never lost. He is not hiding from us. He hasn't gone anywhere. He always has been and always will be everywhere, including inside each person. If someone gave you a present, wrapped in fancy paper and bows, you wouldn't know what was inside until you opened it, would you? That gift could sit for months or even years on your shelf. But as long as you left it unopened, you would not be able to appreciate the gift. It would still be there, waiting inside the box, but it wouldn't be doing you any good.

Our Thoughts Lead to God

This is the way it is with God. He's always within us, waiting for us to discover Him. And the way we discover Him is by thinking about Him and by seeing Him all around us. We can start to feel God's presence in us and appreciate all the splendid things He does.

Your mind is your link with God. With your mind you *think* about God, and you *feel* His love, power, and goodness. So you find God by using your mind to look inside yourself.

And you might be happy to know that anyone who searches for God always finds Him. You can find Him too, now that you know where to look.

How Do I Pray ?

Talk or Think to God

Prayer is talking to God. We can do this out loud or silently. It doesn't matter. What does matter is whether we really mean what we say. It doesn't do much good to repeat a lot of words that we aren't even thinking about. The important thing in prayer is to really *feel* what we are saying.

Some people think prayer is used for begging God to give them something or asking Him to change something in their lives. But this is not the purpose of prayer, because God has already given us everything. We just may not realize it yet.

Why do we pray then? Because when we do pray, something happens to change *us,* and when *we* change, everything else gets better.

When we pray and feel that we are making contact with God (who, remember, is always inside of us), we are resting in what is called the *secret place of the Most High.* We sense we are in the presence of God, and we can talk with Him and bring our problems to Him so that He can give us the answers.

We come to God in our prayer time so that we can let Him work through us. We know He will always make the right things happen.

God's way is not always ''our'' way. God's idea of what is right and best is always perfect; ours may not be. We pray so that God's way will be done. He is never wrong.

God Never Changes

Wouldn't it be terrible if God were someone or something we could influence and bend to our own wishes and ideas? Imagine what kind of God that would be! Every time someone begged for something God would change His mind and do all sorts of foolish things. We certainly wouldn't want a God like that, would we?

But, fortunately, God never changes. It is we who change. God has already given us everything He can give. He has already done for us everything He can do. Now it is up to us to use it and let all of God's perfect goodness do its work in our lives.

Our prayers, then, should be conversations with God in which we tell Him how much we love and appreciate Him. We should tell Him how we want to know more about Him, and be able to see Him everywhere. We should use our prayer time to make that contact with our Creator. When we do, *we* change—not God.

Have you talked to God lately? He is always there, ready to listen to you. He is always ready to meet you at the secret place of the Most High. You can go there anytime you want to. Talk to God. Tell Him how you feel about things. Speak to God as if He were your very best and closest friend, because He is. There is no secret too secret to tell God. There is nothing you cannot share with Him. You can trust Him completely with your most private and special thoughts and feelings. And there is no problem too difficult for God to solve. He will always take care of things in the best possible way if you will turn over the problem to Him so that He can work it out for you. Try it. You'll see that it is true!

And never forget to tell God you are glad He is there, that you love Him, and that you know He always does the right thing.

That is how you pray.

How Much Do You Believe?

You bet God answers prayer! Always. But in order for you to understand this, you must know the difference between wishes and prayer.

Prayer is attached to a *belief* you have deep inside you. For instance, let's say you think you are getting a cold. But deep down you *know* that you cannot be sick, because God is your perfect health. Your prayer of thanks for being well will be answered because it is based on a true belief.

On the other hand, let's suppose you say a prayer to become well, but all the time you are secretly believing you are sick and expect to even get worse. What happens then? Your true prayer was your belief in sickness, and so it is answered! The prayer which you might have *said* about getting well was meaningless because it was not backed up by your beliefs. It was not really a prayer at all, only some wishful thinking.

Do you see the difference? Real, true prayer—supported by our real, true beliefs—is always answered. The next time you pray, check yourself to see if it is a true prayer. Are you expressing a real belief or merely saying empty words?

Get On God's Wavelength

Prayer is talking to God. Meditation is *listening* to God. Both are wonderful experiences. But, by meditating we learn to hear the still small voice that comes from deep within us and brings us guidance. This is the voice of God in us. It is always there to help us. It is usually more like a feeling or knowing than a voice.

Meditation is getting on God's wavelength. It is like listening to a radio. We tune in to His presence. We all should do it at least once a day.

How do you meditate? First you sit in a comfortable chair with your feet flat on the floor and your hands resting on your lap. Close your eyes, and take a few slow, deep breaths. Let each part of your body relax and "melt" into a restful feeling. You are in a state of quiet listening.

Now put your attention on your awareness of God's presence all around you and in you. Sense His great love for you and for all creation. Feel the joy of knowing you are one with God and that there are no limits to your life.

With practice it will become very easy for you to tune in to God. Meditation is the best way to maintain our contact with Him and to receive His guidance. Meditation helps us to always know the right thing to do. When we meditate every day we are able to more and more bring the feelings of our oneness with God (which we get in meditation) into our daily activities. This is important.

Begin today to set aside some time to meditate—to listen to God. Make it a daily habit. God wants you to know Him, so use your meditation periods to hear what His still small voice has to say to you.

Remember—prayer is the time *you* talk; meditation is the time *God* talks. What has God said to you today?

Who Is Jesus ?

He Felt His Oneness with God

Jesus was a man born in Bethlehem almost two thousand years ago. He, more than anyone who has ever lived, felt He was one with God. He sensed the force of God within Him and knew that with God all things are possible.

Because He understood God so perfectly, Jesus was able to do many things that seemed like miracles. But He taught that we, too, can do these things if we put God first.

Jesus came to show us how to be perfect. He showed us how to think, pray, and act. He taught us the Truth, and His teachings are just as perfect and just as valid for us today as they were for His followers many centuries ago.

Jesus does not want us to worship Him. He wants us to do as He did and worship God.

The man Jesus of Nazareth was put to death on a Cross because people didn't understand Him and His teachings. But He was so aware of His oneness with God that He was able to bring His body back to life.

His Deeds Are Not Impossible for Us

When you read about Jesus and the wonderful things He did, do they seem almost impossible to you? Well, you need to begin to realize that what one

39

human being (Jesus) can do, any human being (you) can do! Think about that, because it is true. If we follow Jesus' teachings, we will know our own oneness with God, just as He did. That is His hope for the entire world.

When was the last time you read some of Jesus' words? Read the four gospels in the New Testament of the Bible. Read them slowly so that you get the real message behind each story Jesus tells. How does each story apply in your own life? What is Jesus saying? What is His lesson for you?

Here is a good thing to do each time you wonder how to act or what to say: Try to do what Jesus would do in your place! What would He say, and what would He do?

Let's say, for example, that your feelings are hurt because you feel that someone treated you unfairly or said something unkind to you. Instead of pouting or getting angry, you can decide to act the way Jesus would. Jesus would tell you that another person's less-than-perfect behavior is that person's problem, not yours. Jesus would know that He has nothing to concern Himself with except how He acts toward others. Try to feel how Jesus would act in your particular situation. This will always be your best guide.

We say that Jesus is our Way-Shower. Let His thoughts and words and acts show you the way.

Who or What Is Christ ?

Each of Us Has a Perfect Part

There is part of you that is perfect and unchanging. This is the part that is the essence of God. It is the "real" you. We call it the *Christ* self.

Everyone is familiar in some way with dolls. Children usually have several different sets of clothes that can be put on a doll. Each change of clothes brings a different look to the doll, doesn't it? The outer look of the doll can be changed to fit any occasion. But no matter what clothes you put on it, the doll itself never changes, does it? It always remains the same. Perhaps you can think of your Christ self in a similar way—*it* doesn't change either, no matter how many different ways you act on the outside. The real you—that Christ self—is always perfect.

You should always try to express your Christ self. Jesus was able to identify so completely with His Christ self—His God nature—that He was called Jesus Christ. But Christ is your real name, too. Each of us has a Christ self.

The Christ Is Your Real Self

The Christ in every individual is sometimes called the I AM. The Christ in you is what makes you the wonderful and unique individual that you are. It is the divine part of you. We should let our Christ selves shine out to others, and we should always recognize that same Christ nature in everyone else.

Christ is not a person. *Jesus* is the person. Christ is the God part of Him—and of you and of all people.

You will always know when you are speaking and acting from your Christ self. Are you trying to express your Christ self more often? Are you seeing the beautiful Christ self in everyone else?

What Is the Holy Spirit?

God Has a Moving Force

When God acts out an idea created in His mind, we call that action the Holy Spirit. It is the part of God that created the universe and each of us. It is the moving force that makes God's plan happen.

You know that nothing happens to an idea—no matter how excellent it might be—until you actually do something about it. It is the same with God. His ideas must be expressed in the world. It is the Holy Spirit that does this work.

But we shouldn't think that the Holy Spirit is something separate from God. Not at all. If you have an idea to paint a picture and then you paint that picture, who does the work? It is still you, isn't it? It is the Holy Spirit part of God that does *His* work. But it is still all God.

Holy Spirit Is God in Action

It is the Holy Spirit part of God that you hear speaking to you in your meditation, and it is the Holy Spirit part of God that keeps you alive. We can say then that the Holy Spirit is *God in action.*

See if you can find several examples of the Holy Spirit at work. Evidence of the Holy Spirit is all around you. Train your eyes to see more of it and your ears to hear more of it. Let's appreciate all of the things God does.

What Is the Bible?

The Greatest Book Ever Written

The Bible is made up of sixty-six separate books written by many people who understood the wonders of God or who realized the great Truth that each of us must find. Have you heard people say that the Bible is the greatest book ever written? It is. But do you know why?

The Bible is a record of historical events and a collection of legends from different civilizations, but it is far more to us than that. The Bible is important to us mostly because it is a record of each person's individual search for God.

We are learning to know that we are one with God. Eventually all people will know that. As we go in the direction of expressing more of our Christ selves, we gradually wake up to the fact that God is within us. We start out like Adam, who was not aware of his Christ self, and we work toward becoming like Jesus, who recognized His oneness with God. The Bible begins with Adam and ends with Christ. It is really the record of your own progress. That is why when you read the Bible you should always discover what it is saying to *you*.

The Meaning Behind the Words

The stories and events are symbols of what happens in your own life. Therefore, the Bible can mean something different to each person.

When we read it this way, looking for how it applies to our own lives, we say we are interpreting the Bible *metaphysically*. This means we are looking for the real ideas behind the words and what they represent to us personally.

It can be a lot of fun to read the Bible and interpret it metaphysically. It also can give us a lot of insight into our own thoughts and behavior when we look at it this way.

Plan to open the Bible soon and see how it shows you something about your own search for God. Pick out some of the stories in the Old Testament (like the Tower of Babel or the Flood or Cain and Abel) and try to see what they represent in your life. The more you interpret the Bible this new way, the easier it becomes. Read the Bible and try to discover how every story contains aspects of your own character.

When you read the Bible like this, it always has something new to say to you. There are layers and layers of meaning that are always there for you to discover. As *you* change, the meanings in the Bible stories change. That is why we say the Bible is a living thing and not some outdated collection of religious writings. The Bible will always have deep meanings for us because it contains the great Truths, which are timeless.

God's Laws

Many Laws Are Part of One Big Law

Although we speak about the *laws* of God as if there were many, they all are parts of the one big law of God—the Law of Cause and Effect. *Cause and effect* means that for every effect or result or thing that exists, there is a cause—something made it happen. This also means that the right effect always follows its cause. Everything in the world happened (and is happening) as a result of a specific cause. Let's look at this a little more closely and see some examples of the Law of Cause and Effect.

Examples of the Law

When you eat good, nourishing food, your body grows strong and healthy. Good food was the cause, and good health was the effect. It is part of God's law that your body was designed to run on nutritious food. If you try to go against God's law (in this case the law of nutrition), you set up the *cause* of improper nourishment, and you end up with poor health as the *effect*.

Let's take another example. We know we must never take anything that is not ours. If we do, we set up a *cause* that will eventually bring us a bad *effect*. You see, the law always works. It cannot help itself from working. Whenever someone tries to break God's law, the results are never good.

We Can Count on His Laws

It's nice to know that we can always count on God's laws to work. We can count on receiving happiness and good in our lives when we set the cause of love and kindness, for instance, into motion. You probably have heard it said that what you sow you reap. This idea is taken from the Bible, and it means that whatever kind of cause we plant in our lives will be exactly the kind of results we can expect to get. Good makes good and bad makes bad. The law is very simple, isn't it?

If you planted some radish seeds, you would certainly expect to get radishes and not apples, because the seeds grow according to law. All the miraculous things that take place inside your body operate by the law; each part knows what to do and how to do it. A heart doesn't act like an eye, does it? No, because it follows the law that made it a heart and tells it what a heart is supposed to do.

Our Earth revolves around the sun according to law, and our seasons change according to law. Everywhere we look we see the workings of God's laws.

The Law Works on Thoughts, Too

But God's laws do not operate only with the things we see. There is nothing that is not subject to the law. It is important to know that God's laws operate through your thoughts, too!

For instance, if you think happy thoughts most of the time, you will have happy things all around you in your life. If you believe you are intelligent, you will receive good grades; the law operates to see that you do well in your work.

One of the most important lessons you can ever learn is this: *Everything, including our thoughts and health and events in our lives, operates according to God's laws, and these laws are always perfect and cannot be broken.* God's laws always work! Can you see any examples of the Law of Cause and Effect in your world?

I Create with My Thoughts and Words

We Each Take on Responsibility

You are the king or queen of your world! You have complete authority over your life. That is a most ideal position in which to be, isn't it? *You* are in control.

But, as with any ruler, along with the power comes a large responsibility. Not only do you have to be willing to take command, but you also have to be willing to accept the full responsibility for your decisions. In other words, you must take responsibility for all of the causes you have set into motion. (Remember the Law of Cause and Effect?)

Thoughts and Words Have Royal Power

The power of your ruling ability lies mainly in two very important areas: your thoughts and your words. Thoughts and words are the means by which you build your kingdom. They have creative power and, when you really *believe* what you think and say, your thoughts and words go forth as loyal subjects to do the bidding of their ruler, which is you!

Now we know that there are good kings and not-so-good kings. Since the king or queen is in complete command of the kingdom, his assistants must obey his orders at all times. If he issues a good command, the result will be good. If he issues a poor command, the results will be less than desirable. (It is our old friend the Law of Cause and Effect again.) In other words, the command is always carried out exactly according to the royal decree.

Your thoughts and words act in the same way as a king's decree. They go forth to create with your royal power. You, as supreme ruler of your thoughts and words, have total command over what direction they take. A less-than-good thought can always be replaced by a good, constructive thought. A less-than-good word can always be rendered powerless by speaking good words. It is as simple as that.

Our thoughts and words should always reflect our *true* selves—the Christ within us. That same power that we sometimes use so destructively in our thoughts and words can be turned around and used constructively for *good* results.

You must remember that you alone are responsible for the things in your kingdom. Are you using your royal powers wisely, or are you wasting them? Start noticing what kind of decrees your thoughts and words are sending forth.

Yes and No

It All Begins in the Mind

We know, don't we, that everything begins in the mind? The mind is where we store our feelings, thoughts, and beliefs about people and things. And we also know that, since everything works according to the law, whatever we have in our minds is going to come forth into our world. (We meet again our old friend the Law of Cause and Effect! He certainly gets around, doesn't he?)

We often say the mind is the soil in which we grow our world. Can you see how important it is to plant the right things? And can you see how important it is to have the right soil if your garden is going to grow the way you want it to? If you wanted to grow some flowers, you would first have to pull all the weeds, otherwise they would crowd out the flowers and keep them from growing properly. After all the weeds were pulled, you could plant your flowers.

You prepare your mind for good thoughts in much the same way. You first have to get rid of the straggly weeds that might be growing there. These weeds could be things like hate, fear, jealousy, resentment, selfishness, or anything else that gets in the way of your being the Christ person you are meant to be.

Denials

We can get rid of these weeds of the mind by using what we call *denials*.

Denials are statements that deny the existence of unchristlike things. An example of a denial is: *There is nothing for me to fear.* Or: *I cannot inherit illness.* Or: *I am not a poor student.* You can make up your own denials for any situation that seems to be holding you apart from God. A denial is a way of saying, "No!"

When you come up with a good, strong denial to fit your situation, use it many times a day. Say it aloud when you can, and say it silently whenever you think of it. This is the way you pull those weeds that you must get rid of before you can plant your garden.

But what would happen if you got rid of all those weeds that have been hindering you and you didn't do anything else with your garden? Pretty soon those pesty weeds would be springing up again, wouldn't they? We know that once we pull the weeds the soil must be planted with the flowers.

Our minds work the same way. After we have done the work with our denials, we must "plant the flowers." We do this with what we call *affirmations*.

Affirmations

Affirmations are strong statements that state Truth, about ourselves or a situation. Since Truth is that God is in every situation, the affirmation should reflect this. For instance, some affirmations could be: *I am intelligent, I am well and strong, I am filled with love,* or *I am calm and peaceful.* You can make up affirmations to fit your own needs.

An affirmation is a way of saying, "Yes!" The only rule to follow is that your affirmation must be based on Truth. Then it works to establish whatever it is you are decreeing. (Can you guess what law this is following?) It would do no good, for instance, to affirm that cigarettes are good for you when they work against God's laws for health. Or it would do no good to affirm that you cannot be hurt and then jump in front of a train!

Do you understand the principle—the main idea—behind affirmations? They *must* be based on Truth. But when they are, and when we use them over and over each day, they become powerful aids to the improvement of ourselves and our kingdoms.

What kind of garden is your mind? Is it full of weeds, or is it filled with flowers? If your garden needs work, get busy with the two best tools you can use—denials and affirmations. See how beautiful you can make your garden!

There Is Good in Everything

God Is in the Midst of Everything

This is important for you to learn: *There is good in everything.* That might seem difficult to believe, because most of us are in the habit of judging many situations and people in our lives as ''bad.''

It may seem difficult to think of a broken leg, measles, failing grades, or being robbed as having good in them. But they do. Do you wonder how this can be true? It is quite simple: God is in the midst of everything. There is no place in the universe where God is not present.

What do we do, then, when we are faced with something that appears to be less than good? We remember the Truth that God is everywhere and that God is good. Then we start looking for God in the situation; we start looking for good. If we look hard enough, we will always find it.

Sometimes the good does not show right away. We must be patient and trust God's perfect plan. Eventually God will show Himself, and we will see how something we thought was bad really brought good into the world.

Here Are Some Examples of This Truth

Let's go back to our original examples of what we said might seem to be negative situations. An unhappy, overweight woman who broke her leg became so impressed with her exercises to strengthen the leg that she started on a total fitness program and eventually found much happiness as a slim, healthy person. A young boy home in bed with measles was watching a daytime television program on oceanography. He became so fascinated with the subject that he later made it his career. A young man flunked out of college. He never studied, and had gone to college in the first place only because his parents had wanted him to go. After several years of growing and becoming wiser, he later returned to college because *he* wanted to attend. He now appreciated his education and graduated with honors. A widow whose house was burglarized later married the police investigator of her case.

There is no situation or person so ''bad'' that God is not present. Look back at some of the things in the past that seemed so terrible and see what good came out of them. Why not make a game of seeing God in every person and every situation? Let it become a habit with you. If we believe in God, we have to trust Him to let the right thing always happen. Good comes out of ''bad'' every time. Start looking for it now.

Don't React

No One Can Hurt Us in Any Way

We discovered in our last lesson that God is present in every situation. Once we learn that lesson thoroughly we will no longer get upset or angry if something seems to go wrong. We won't even be disappointed in people or let our feelings be hurt by them. It is our *reactions* that allow us to be hurt. If someone says something that you don't like, what does it matter? His anger (or jealousy or whatever) is *his* problem—not yours. You don't have to accept it or let it bother you.

When we look to other people or things to make us happy, we put our hopes and expectations in the wrong place. There is only one place to look for happiness, and that is inside ourselves. We have to learn to turn to our Christ selves, which will *never* disappoint us. That is the only thing upon which we can really rely, because it is always perfect. That is why prayer and meditation are important—they keep us tuned in to our true selves.

Have you been reacting to everyone and everything in your world, giving all of it permission to affect you? It doesn't have to be that way. You can begin looking to your own Christ nature as your source of happiness.

This doesn't mean that we ignore others or are unkind to them. Certainly not. It means that we love everyone and see God at work everywhere. It means that we always do our best. And when we do, we have done our share and can know that we have done God's will. That is all *we* have to worry about. What others do and say is *their* responsibility and not ours.

More Examples of Truth

The bully in the schoolyard, the teacher who seems to yell at everyone, the little brother who doesn't want to share his toys—these really don't have anything to do with you. Each is doing what he feels he must do at the time. But his words and actions should have no effect on you, because they really have nothing to do with you. Your job is only to do your best. Your job is to think, speak, and act from your perfect Christ self, which loves everyone and sees that same Christ in everyone else.

This is a difficult lesson for some of us to learn. But when we do learn it, we find that our lives are changed. We are much happier, and things generally seem to work out perfectly.

We Must Not Condemn Others

Condemning Others Is Not Godlike

Have you ever noticed that whenever you say something bad about somebody you have a feeling way down deep inside that lets you know you shouldn't have done it? Before you condemn somebody, notice that little feeling telling you not to do it. Do you know what that feeling is? It is your own Christ self, the perfect part of you, which wants you to do only Godlike things. Condemning others is not Godlike.

Can you guess why it is wrong? Think back to what you have already learned. God is everywhere. He is in all places and in all people. Each person has a Christ self which is perfect because it is part of God. So if we condemn someone, we are condemning a part of God, aren't we? And we certainly do not want to do that.

Remember we learned that we have to take care of only our own thoughts, words, and actions. What others do is their responsibility. Each person is doing the very best he can do, and we must not criticize him if it seems to us he should be doing something else.

We Cannot Know Best for Others

The truth is that we cannot possibly know what is best for anyone other than ourselves. God is working through everyone, and we have no right to judge harshly or to condemn. We would not want others to do it to us, would we? And we should not do it to them.

This is one of the important teachings of Jesus. He told us that we must not judge others. If we do, we can expect the Law of Cause and Effect to bring poor results back to us. Think about it.

Try to become aware of each time you want to criticize someone. Then stop before you do. Soon you will be seeing God in everyone, and who would want to condemn God?

Let's Talk About Forgiveness

Don't Take Troubles to Tomorrow

We should never go to sleep at night feeling angry or resentful toward anyone. Each evening the slate should be wiped clean so that we don't carry any bad feelings over into the next day.

If we feel we have to forgive someone, it means that we judged him harshly or condemned him, doesn't it? If we had never judged that he did something ''wrong,'' there would be nothing to forgive. In other words, we didn't keep our eyes on the God in that person. We decided that he did something we have to forgive.

If we can learn this, we will have the answer to many seeming problems in our lives. Once we realize that God is in everyone, we see that there is nothing to forgive, and the blocks to our own happiness are removed.

Forgive and Forget

If we say that we will forgive someone but we won't forget what he did, we are not seeing God in him. Or if we say we will forgive him even if he was wrong, we are still not seeing God in him. It all boils down to this: That person is as much a part of God as you are. There is nothing to forgive if you do not condemn him in the first place.

We Need to Forgive Ourselves

But there is *someone* to forgive, and that is yourself! Yes. If you have had feelings against another person it is *you* who must be forgiven! "Forgive me for not forgiving you."

If there is someone in your life who you feel has wronged you, realize that he is part of God and so there is nothing to criticize and nothing to forgive. You need to ask his forgiveness of you.

We can ask forgiveness of others in two ways. Either we can go to that person directly and ask his forgiveness, or we can mentally ask him during our meditation periods. Both ways work. In meditation we can even apologize to people who are dead.

"Forgive *me*." That is the only forgiving that needs to be done. Try it. It works every time.

It's Good to Be Thankful

God Gives Us Everything

If you stop and think about it, you will realize that God has given us everything there is to give! Everything! God has given us so much that we are unable to know it all. It is God's very nature to give and give and give.

So many marvelous and beautiful things are evidence of God's giving. And He has even given us all the wonderful things we cannot see, like love, wisdom, health, and imagination. We are so used to all of God's gifts everywhere around us that we sometimes forget to be thankful for them. We take them for granted.

But this is a mistake, because it is only when we express our thanks for something that we are able to have its full benefit. When we are thankful for something it means we are aware of it. And it is not until we are aware of something that we can use it properly.

Thankfulness Increases Our Good

When we are thankful for something, that thing increases and becomes even more useful to us. If you have ever trained a puppy to do tricks or to be obedient, you know that it performed best when you praised it and showed your gratitude. Everything in life responds to the power of praise and thanksgiving.

We give thanks for our nourishing food, and it does its good work in our bodies. We give thanks for our money before we place it in the church offering plate, knowing that our thanks for it will help its benefits to increase. We can praise and thank our bicycles, toys, clothes, and automobiles so that they will serve us better. Scientists have even shown that praising plants will make them grow better!

If you want to see even more good things in your life, praise what you have. Be thankful for it. Look about you for all the things God has given you, and then let Him know you are grateful.

I Am Prosperous

Believe You Are Wealthy, and You Will Be

Do you know people who are always worried about money? These people are always complaining that they never have enough. And do you know what? As long as they believe it, they never will!

People who are always concerned about their money have not yet learned that God is the source of their supply. When we realize that God wants to give us everything we need in order to be happy, we will stop worrying and begin to accept God's goodness.

But we don't sit back and do nothing and expect God to hand us everything. No. We have our part to play, and that is that we must put God first in all things. It is called *practicing the presence of God*. We practice feeling God's presence all around us at all times. Then we think and do things that will express the God part of us. We will always want to do God's will—what He wants us to do. (We discover God's will when we listen to Him during our meditations.)

When we are doing God's will—always trying to become a better person and always being loving and helpful to those around us—we will be doing the things that bring us the riches of God. Whatever we need will come to us. If we need money to help us do more and better things for God, we will have money. If we need wisdom, we will have wisdom. If we need love, we will have love. Whatever we need we will have when we live according to God's will.

We say that there is a "substance" everywhere, out of which everything is formed. It is formed into whatever "molds" we provide.

The Clay Becomes the Shape of the Mold

If you have some modeling clay and want to form it into something, you press it into a mold. Whatever the shape your mold is, that is the shape the clay will become, won't it? The original clay is formless. It has no definite shape. It is waiting to be put into the mold so it can be formed into something real and useful to you. It is not until you press the clay into that mold that it becomes "something." And you know that it must become exactly what the mold is.

This brings us back again to the Law of Cause and Effect. When we are thinking and doing good things, we are creating a mold of goodness for God's substance.

We never have to worry or wonder about how God's substance comes into our lives. No one can really understand God's ways yet—they are too advanced for most of us. All we have to know is that God *always* keeps His part of the bargain when we keep ours. We just have to have faith that our good will come—and it will!

So never doubt that you are rich with all of God's wealth. God wants to give you everything you need. Use the tools of your thoughts and words (the molds) to shape His substance into good things. This is using the Law of Cause and Effect correctly. It always works.

God Doesn't Know About Sickness

We Must Believe We are Healthy

God's idea for you is perfect. He created you with all the things you need in order to be strong and healthy. And He gave you all the laws you need to obey if you want to stay healthy.

Any illness is just a less-than-perfect state of health, and it was certainly not created by God. Anytime we seem to be less than what God created us to be—whether in areas of health, wisdom, finances, or anything else—we are separating ourselves from the God inside us, which is the real and perfect part of us.

To be healthy we must think and believe that we are healthy. We have to know that we are part of God, and God is perfect. If God is perfect, He can never be sick, can He? Therefore, neither can we.

But again, as always, God asks that we do our share. He has created us to function according to certain laws He made for us. When it comes to our health, there are God's laws of nutrition and exercise and rest which we must obey. Remember that everything in the universe works by laws. That is what makes order, beauty, and perfection.

Without laws there would be terrible confusion everywhere. But God's laws control everything, and we should be very thankful that they do.

God Lives Within Each of Us

The body is called the temple of the living God. God lives in us and, because He does, we want to keep our temples beautiful and well, don't we? We don't want to hurt or destroy our temples by putting wrong foods and drinks into them or not exercising them or not resting them properly.

Because God lives in you, you will want to give Him the very best home that you possibly can. When you obey His laws of nutrition, exercise, and rest, God can do His share to keep you in perfect health.

Are you obeying His laws? With what kind of foods and drinks are you building your temple? Do you get enough exercise and rest? Let's give God the very best temples we can. He deserves them, doesn't He?

Love Holds the World Together

Love Is Everywhere, in Everything

Some people say that love is the universal glue! Love is the strongest attracting power in all creation. It binds us all together as one great and marvelous union—all part of the one God. God *is* love. And this love pulls us all toward our true Christ selves, making us more and more like God.

It is love that holds together the molecules of iron to make them into a frying pan, and it is love that holds the planets in their orbits and us in our forms as human beings. Love is everywhere.

Love at all Times

But sometimes we humans use our ability to love only at certain times and on certain people. We feel we can love only those people who love us or who are the same as we are. But this is not using our wonderful power of love in the correct way. The truth is that everyone is like us because we are all united as part of God. The same God that is in you is in every other person, no matter how it may seem to be otherwise.

If we are going to live the way God designed us to, we will have to love everyone. To love less than that is not to love God. It is important to always keep our attention on the Christ nature of each person, not on outer appearances.

Our Love Should Go to Everyone

When we let the warmth of our love flow out from us in a complete circle, we touch everyone with it, and the world becomes a better place. We meet each person Christ-to-Christ and automatically let our love reach him. To love in God's way we have to let it flow freely, not withholding it from anyone.

Think of the people in your life whom you love the most. Feel the love which fills you when you think of these people. It's a good and wonderful feeling, isn't it? Well, this is the feeling we should have for *all* people. We need to love the person who took something from us just as much as we love our best friend. This may seem difficult to do. But when you realize that everyone wants to be loved, and that everything he does is his way of crying out for that love, you begin to feel your own love moving in his direction. It takes a lot of practice to love everybody, but this is the way God loves us, and it is the way He desires us to be too.

Love is a mighty magnet. Whatever we love we attract into our lives. If we love God we will attract goodness. Eventually each of us will have to realize that he is part of everyone else. And he must love everyone because we are all one.

What are you loving? Are you holding your love back in places? Try letting it beam out in a complete circle like a candle or a bright light, falling on everyone and everything in its path. People will notice your radiance and will love you in return.

What Is This Thing Called Faith?

If We Believe We Can, We Can

Maybe the simplest definition of faith is this: Faith is acting on what you believe. Whatever you really believe in, you will act on. You have faith in it.

You believe that you can stand up on your two legs and so you do. You have faith in your ability to stand up. You believe that you can ride a bicycle, and so you ride your bicycle. You have faith in your ability to ride a bicycle. You don't believe that you can fly like a bird, do you? So you don't fly. You have no faith in an ability to fly.

God wants us to have faith in Him. He wants us to have faith that our lives will be happy, healthy, and prosperous. If we really believe this is true, then we will act as if it were true.

When we have faith in something, we know that it is true. It doesn't matter what it may look like on the outside. Real faith is based on an inner knowing, not on outer conditions. But we can tell if we really have faith in something by the way we act.

Our Actions Tell Us Where Our Faith Is

If we say we believe that we inherit perfect health from God (which we do), and then go around complaining about a headache or eating the wrong foods, we do not have real faith in God's health do we? Our actions always reveal where our true faith lies.

When we practice meditation each day, we will come to know more of God's Truth. The more we know and believe of this Truth, the more we will act as if it were so.

Where is your faith? Is it in poor health or failing grades or unhappy relationships with people? Or is your faith in Truth? Check to see what your actions are telling you. They will show you where your faith is. And if it seems to be in the wrong things, make an effort to know the real Truth and put your faith in that.

Our faith belongs with God and His goodness for us. Then we will act on this belief and our lives will be beautiful.

Why Am I Here ?

God Reveals Himself Through Us

Do you remember at the beginning of this book we said that the question "why am I here?" is probably one of the two biggest questions we can ever ask? Have you been thinking about it as you've read the book? Perhaps by now you have come up with some good answers of your own to this important question. Everyone wants to know why he is here on this planet Earth. These ideas might help you to find the answer.

When we let the perfect Christ part of us think and speak and act, we are letting God come forth. He has created us and wants to express Himself through us. This is the best way God can show Himself to the world—through us.

Each of us is a perfect part of God's plan for the world. You express God in your own individual way, and only you can play that particular part. It is up to you to express your own true nature—the God part of you. You are necessary to God's plan, and He has given you everything you need to become perfect.

Jesus said we must become as perfect as God. And we can. That is why God made us. He wants each of us to live perfectly. When we think or say or do something that is less than Godlike, we are not fulfilling our purpose in life.

Does being perfect sound like an impossible goal? It really isn't. Jesus did it and so can you. Begin by knowing that there is only one thing in this whole world, and that is God. And God is good. God created you as a part of His great plan for the world. He needs you.

It Takes Everyone to Make Our World

Have you ever put together a jigsaw puzzle? If you have, you know there are many pieces of all different shapes, and the picture is not complete until you have put the last piece in place. The picture would not be perfect without each section. In the same way, each person is a piece of God's universe. Each of us is different from the others, but it takes everyone to make the plan complete.

So you must start being aware that you are necessary to God's plan and that His hopes for you are very high. He wants you to be perfect.

Next, you can keep a close watch on the thoughts that come into your mind. Are they worthwhile thoughts? Will they create goodness? If a negative, not-so-good thought pops up, do you push it aside right away and replace it with a better one? Sometimes we might have an un-Godlike thought pop up. This can happen. But the trick is to get rid of it at once so it can do no harm to us.

And what about your words—are they always spoken from your Christ self? If they are, you know they have the power to create a lot of good. We should always try to make our words the kindest and most loving and helpful that we can.

Check Out Your Actions

The last thing we can check is our actions. What kind of things are we doing?

Are we expressing our God nature, or are we settling for less?

These are all important ways we can become more like our real selves. Being our real selves is why we are here. Becoming the perfect God person you were created to be should be your greatest goal. Spend some time thinking about this goal and how you are a necessary part of God's gigantic jigsaw puzzle!

You can get help along the way by listening to God in your meditation times. This helps keep you on the right track and makes it easier to work toward your goal.

You are here for a purpose, and that is to be the perfect creation God designed you to be. God's purpose for you is to express Him in your own unique way. And only you can do it! Isn't that exciting!

I Will Become New

God Wants Us to Really Live

Jesus taught that we don't have to die to find heaven—that heaven is right here where we are. We carry heaven around inside of us, but most of us do not know that. Heaven is that feeling of waking up to the fact that we are one with God. We don't have to go anywhere to find it.

God did not invent death or ever create a law that says we must die. God wants us to live and become like Him. In fact, He promises us that when we finally live every minute of every day as the real people we are—letting our Christ selves come out—an amazing thing will happen! This amazing thing is called *regeneration*.

When you have reached the stage where you know at all times that you are one with God and do and say only Godlike things, your whole self will have changed, won't it? All the negative things that were in your life but were not helping you to know God better will have disappeared. Your mind will be different now.

But regeneration—which means a new beginning or a rebirth—extends to the entire physical body as well as the mind. When you become completely at one with God, your body will be changed too. It will be filled with light and never have any weakness or illness. Nothing will be able to hurt or destroy it.

Jesus was regenerated. His body was so filled with light that even the act of crucifying Him could not destroy it.

Marvelous things are in store for you too when you start becoming the perfect God person you were born to be. There is no limit to what you can do.

Only You Can Stop You

Who is the one person in the entire universe who can keep you from being perfect? It's you! You can achieve all of God's greatness, or you can keep yourself from it. It's your choice. Do you pick negative things like anger, fear, hatred, complaining, time-wasting, and illness—or do you choose God?

If you want to do something but someone says you must do something else, do you choose to become angry and sulk, or do you choose to do the task happily because you know it needs to be done? If someone damages something that is yours, do you choose to feel mean toward him and want to get even, or do you choose to give him your love because love and friendship are more important than any possession?

We have choices to make many times every day. What we choose determines what our lives will be like.

Today can be the first day of your new life if you want it to. It can be a real birthday for you—a whole new beginning!

God is waiting for you to recognize Him. He has been right there all the time. Look inside yourself. Don't you think it's time to start being your real and wonderful self? Choose God, and celebrate your real birthday! The best is yet to come. A whole new you is on the way. Happy birthday, child of God!

Printed U.S.A.

156-F-6121-7,500M-3-83